Basic Math

Sharing and Dividing

Richard Leffingwell

Heinemann Library
Chicago, Illinois

Customer Service   888–454–2279
Visit our website at www.heinemannlibrary.com

Photo research by Erica Newbery
Designed by Joanna Hinton- Malivoire
Printed in China by South China Printing Company

10 09 08 07 06
10 9 8 7 6 5 4 3 2 1

Library of Congress Cataloging-in-Publication Data
Leffingwell, Richard.
  Sharing and dividing / Richard Leffingwell.
     p. cm. -- (Basic math)
  Includes bibliographical references and index.
  ISBN 1-4034-8158-X (library binding-hardcover : alk. paper) -- ISBN 1-4034-8163-6 (pbk. : alk. paper)
  1. Division--Juvenile literature. 2. Arithmetic--Juvenile literature. I. Title. II. Series: Leffingwell, Richard. Basic math.
  QA115.L449 2006
  513.2'14--dc22
                      2006005918

Acknowledgments
The author and publisher are grateful to the following for permission to reproduce copyright material: Getty Images (Photodisc Red/Davies & Starr) pp. **4, 5, 6, 7, 8**; Harcourt Education Ltd (www.mmstudios.co.uk) pp. **9–20, 22**, back cover; Photolibrary (Brand X/Burke Triolo) p. **21**

Cover photograph reproduced with permission of Harcourt Education Ltd (www.mmstudios.co.uk)

Contents

What Is Sharing? 4

Sharing Flowers. 9

Sharing Cars 14

Practicing Dividing. 21

Quiz. 22

The "Divided by" Sign 23

Index 24

What Is Sharing?

You and a friend find 6 shells on the beach.

You want to share the shells.

How many shells does each person get?

Pass the shells out one at a time.

Do this until all of the shells
are gone.

Each person gets 3 shells.

They each get a fair share.

$$6 \div 2 = 3$$

Sharing equally is also dividing.

The shells are now divided equally.

Sharing Flowers

What if you had 9 flowers and 3 vases?

How could you divide them equally?

First you put 1 flower in each vase.

You still have 6 flowers left.

Then you put another flower in each vase.

You still have 3 flowers left.

Put another flower in each vase.

Now all of the vases have the same number of flowers.

$$9 \div 3 = 3$$

You divided 9 flowers into 3 vases.

Each vase has 3 flowers.

Sharing Cars

You and a friend have 6 toy cars.

How many will you have if you share them equally?

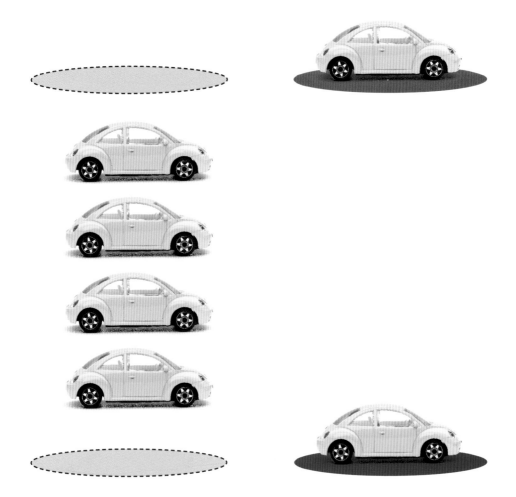

You start by each taking 1 toy car.

There are still 4 toy cars left.

You each take another toy car until they are divided equally.

You each get 3 toy cars.

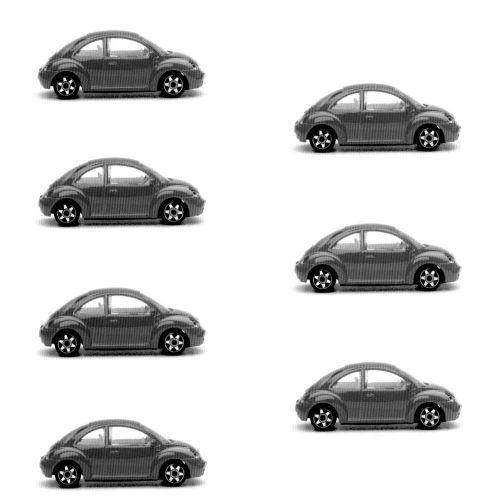

What would you do if you had 7 toy cars to share with your friend?

Each of you would get 3 toy cars.

There would be 1 left over.

What should you do with the extra toy car?

You could give it to another friend.

You could save it until you have another one to share equally.

Practicing Dividing

Now you have divided to share a group of things.

When have you divided things?

Quiz

You have **8** pencils.

How many will there be in each of the 2 pots?

Make sure each pot gets a fair share!

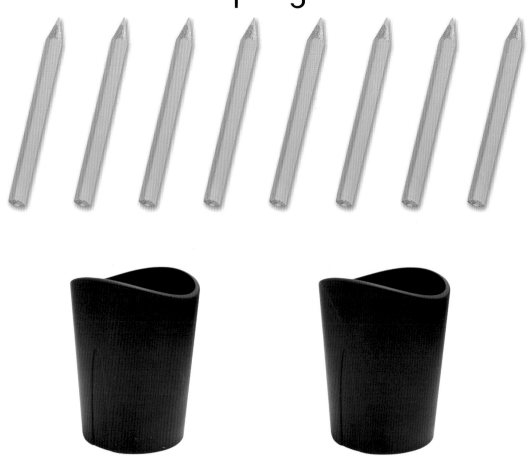

The "Divided by" Sign

| ÷ | You use this sign to show that you are dividing one number by another. |

$$4 \div 2$$

When you divide 4 by 2, you get 2.

| = | You use the equals sign to show what 4 divided by 2 is equal to. |

$$4 \div 2 = 2$$

Index

cars   14, 15, 16, 17, 18, 19
flowers 9, 10, 11, 12, 13
pencils   22
pots   22
shells   4, 5, 6, 7
signs   23
vases   9, 10, 11, 12, 13

Answer to the quiz on page 22
There will be 4 pencils in each pot.

Note to parents and teachers
Reading nonfiction texts for information is an important part of a child's literacy development. Readers can be encouraged to ask simple questions and then use the text to find the answers. Most chapters in this book begin with a question. Read the questions together. Look at the pictures. Talk about what the answer might be. Then read the text to find out if your predictions were correct. To develop readers' enquiry skills, encourage them to think of other questions they might ask about the topic. Discuss where you could find the answers. Assist children in using the contents page, picture glossary, and index to practice research skills and new vocabulary.